# INNOVATORS:

## women in history who have made positive contributions to STEAM

a  let's go full STEAM ahead  book

**written & illustrated by Sierra Marie Bonn**

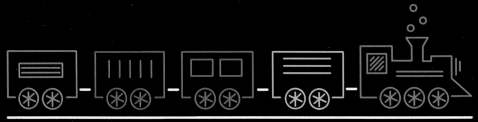

let's go full **STEAM** ahead

In the United States, women make up only 24% of the innovation workforce, according to a 2017 study done by the Department of Commerce.

Women are innovators.

# in·no·va·tor
/ˈinəˌvādər/

*noun*

1. a person who introduces new methods, ideas, or products.
*"She was one of the great innovators in math."*

Women have been introducing methods, ideas, and products into society for thousands of years.

"Let's Go Full STEAM Ahead!" was created to highlight the contributions of women in STEAM (science, technology, engineering, arts, and math).

# S

## science

# "Science is all around us!"
## Camille Schrier, Miss America
## 2020

Science is a massive field of study, ranging from astronomy to zoology. Science is about interacting with the world around us, and asking critical questions about what we observe. The scientists in the next few pages have observed the oceans, the stars, and the human mind.

# Jeanne Villepreux-Power
## *Marine Biologist*

Jeanne Villepreux-Power was born on September 24, 1794 in France, and she invented the glass aquarium. Jeanne's first job was making wedding dresses, and after she got married, she spent years studying marine biology. She made discoveries about various aquatic creatures -- including the argonaut, also known as a paper nautilus. She was the first woman admitted to the Catania Accademia, a fine arts academy in Catania, Sicily, and a crater on Venus (the second planet from the sun) is also named in her honor.

Thank you, Jeanne Villepreux-Power, for your contributions to natural history, marine biology, and for showing women that they can be pioneering scientists and creative fashionistas at the same time!

# Maria Mitchell
## *Astronomer*

Maria Mitchell became fond of the stars at an early age. In 1847, she became the first American astronomer ever to discover a comet. She traveled the world, and was awarded a gold medal from King Frederick VI of Denmark for her services to astronomy. In 1848, she was the first woman elected to the American Academy of Arts and Sciences, and she is thought to be the first professional woman to be hired by the U.S. government.

Maria was also passionate about advocating for science and math education. She started a school for girls interested in math and science when she was just 17, and later on served as the first female professor of astronomy.

Thank you, Maria Mitchell, for your dedication to math and science, and for your inspirational achievements!

# Rita Levi-Montalcini
## *Neurobiologist*

Born in Italy in 1909, Rita was expected to become a proper lady, wife, and mother, and was discouraged to pursue her interests of becoming a doctor. Eventually, her parents realized she had potential and allowed her to attend the University of Turin. There, Rita studied medicine, specifically focusing on neurology.

In 1938, Jewish people in Italy, like Rita, were forbidden to practice medicine due to the anti-Semitic climate of World War II... but Rita didn't stop. She snuck fertilized chicken eggs into her bedroom, and would dissect them to experiment with the nervous system, and the research she did in secret set the stage for her Nobel Prize winning discovery of the Nerve Growth Factor in 1986.

Thank you, Rita Levi-Montalcini, for your dedication to promoting the sciences and for advocating for equality!

# "We are changing the world with technology."
## Bill Gates

Technology can be found in all aspects of life, from telephones and medicine to transportation and marketing. Technology is about innovating the world we live in to make it better for all humankind. The technologists in the next few pages have each made significant contributions that influence our daily lives.

# Ada Lovelace
## Computer Programmer

Augusta Ada Byron King, Countess of Lovelace (or Ada Lovelace, for short) is referred to as the first computer programmer, because of her contributions to an article about Charles Babbage's Analytical Machine, a computing device.

Originally, Ada was just consulted to translate the article from French to English, but ended up extrapolating on the programming ideas so much that her notes and additions are said to have been triple the originalarticle's length. Her mentor, Charles Babbage, called her the "Enchantress of Numbers," for she understood the plans for the computing device as well as Babbage, the creator, but was better at articulating its use and potential.

Every second Tuesday in October, her contributions to the world of computer science and math is honored through Ada Lovelace Day, a celebration of women in STEM around the world.

Thank you, Ada, for your work in mathematics, for creating the field of computer science, and for being a role model for girls everywhere.

# Hedy Lamarr
## *Inventor*

Hedy was born in Austria in 1914, and grew up as an only child. Her father encouraged her to look at the world with an inquisitive eye. He and taught her how machines work, starting a life-long passion for innovation. Her beauty and interests in the arts lead her to the silver screen, and she starred in various films during her lifetime.

Hedy married an Austrian munitions dealer, Fritz Mandl, where she was incredibly unhappy. She was forced to entertain guests and friends of Mandl, many of whom were associated with the Nazi Party, a difficult situation as Hedy was Jewish. After a few years of marriage, she left Mandl in 1937 and went to London -- taking with her the knowledge gained from dinner-table conversation over wartime weaponry.

After spending a few years in Hollywood, and during the onset of World War II, Hedy decided to use her knowledge to advance the Allies' war effort. She worked with George Anthiel, a composer, and the two came up with a new communication system used with the intention of guiding torpedoes to their targets. Hedy was granted a patent in 1942. This technology paved the way for Wi-Fi, Bluetooth, and even GPS -- without Hedy and her inventive spirit, we wouldn't have many of the technologies that make our lives so convenient today!

Thank you, Hedy, for your intelligent mind and for your interdisciplinary interests, and for serving as a role model for women everywhere!

# Grace Hopper
## *Computer Scientist*

Grace Hopper was born in 1906, and from an early age had an insatiable curiosity. At age seven, her mother noticed all the alarm clocks in the house had disappeared -- Grace had disassembled seven of them to learn how they worked and discover why they rang out!

When Grace got older, she attended Vassar College where she earned degrees in mathematics and physics, and Yale University where she received a Ph.D. in mathematics. She then taught at Yale for a time, before leaving to join the U.S. Navy Reserves during World War II. Grace graduated top of her class at the Naval Reserves Midshipmen's School, and was assigned to work on the Bureau of Ships Computation Project at Harvard, where she collaborated with Howard H. Aiken and others on the famous Mark I Computer.

In Grace's time, computers were primarily used to do arithmetic and could only understand symbols, but she had the idea that if data processors could program computers in English, they could do so much more -- and thus COBOL, one of the first and most widely-used data processing languages, was born.

Thank you, Grace, for your work in mathematics and computer science, and for empowering future generations of technologists!

# E

## engineering

**"Successful engineering is all about understanding how things break or fail."**
*Henry Petroski*

Engineering is the act of solving problems, from the large-scale problems, like how to construct a bridge, to the small-scale problems, like how to design a pacemaker. Engineering is about thinking creatively to overcome obstacles. The engineers in this section have studied ways to solve problems in each of their fields.

# Mae Jemison
## *Astronaut*

Born in Alabama and raised in Chicago, Mae was always curious about the world. She told her kindergarten teacher that she wanted to be a scientist, and earned a scholarship to attend Stanford University at just 16 years old. She graduated with degrees in chemical engineering and African and African-American Studies, and pursued her doctorate at Cornell Medical School.

After serving in the Peace Corps for a few years, Mae was inspired by the first woman astronaut, Sally Ride, and by her own life-long love of Star Trek, to pursue her childhood dream. In 1992, she was the first African-American to go into space, flying on the space shuttle Endeavor, where she was the co-investigator of two bone cell research experiments.

Dr. Jemison has since created the Jemison Group, a consulting company that encourages science, tech, and social change. She has also established The Dorothy Jemison Foundation for Excellence, named for her mother, and continues to advocate for minorities in STEM and promote educational opportunities for all.

Thank you, Dr. Jemison, for your work to include people in STEAM fields, for your service as a doctor and scientist, and for being an inspiration to young women across the world!

# Amelia Earhart
## *Aviator*

Amelia Earhart was born in Atchison, Kansas in 1897, and was entranced by the thought of flying. As a child, she and her sister would explore the neighborhood, collecting worms and grasshoppers and building homemade ramps, which she used to fly through the air, often coming to a crash landing. Amelia always aspired to pursue a career in male-dominated fields, and had kept a scrapbook with newspaper clippings that detailed success stories of accomplished women.

Her first flight, in 1920, cost $10 and lasted only ten minutes. From then on, Amelia knew she needed to fly. She saved $1,000 for flight school, and eventually became a world-renowned aviator. She was the first woman to fly solo across the Atlantic Ocean, and she set numerous flying records. Amelia used her talents and experience with planes on the ground, too, teaching and advising women in aeronautical engineering at Purdue University. In 1937, Amelia attempted to fly around the world, and ultimately, disappeared.

Thank you, Amelia, for pursuing and excelling in a male-dominated career, and for showing young girls around the world that they can, too!

# Edith Clarke
## *Electrical Engineer*

Edith was orphaned at twelve years old, but she didn't let her struggles stop her. She became the first woman to graduate with a Masters' in electrical engineering from MIT, and the first female professor of electrical engineering. Edith also invented the Clarke Calculator, a device capable of computing electric current, voltage, and impedance in power transmission lines, earning her a place in the National Inventors Hall of Fame.

She worked for General Electric for many years as both a mathematical computer and as an electrical engineer. She was the first woman to deliver a paper at the American Institute of Electrical Engineers' annual meeting and became the first female fellow of the organization.

Thank you, Edith, for your innovative contributions to the field of electrical engineering!

# A

## arts

## "I think there's an artist hidden in the bottom of every single one of us."
### *Bob Ross*

Art can be expressed through paintings, words, music, pictures, sculptures, plays, and many other mediums. Art is using creativity to express yourself and to share your interpretation of the world around you. The artists in the next few pages share their creativity through singing songs, playing the violin, and performing on stage.

# Manami Ito
## *Violinist*

Manami Ito began playing the violin at just seven years old. She wanted to be a nurse when she grew up, and went to college to pursue medicine. Her academic plans were put on hold in 2004, when she was in a traffic accident. The accident caused her to lose her arm, but she didn't let that stop her. She became the first nurse in all of Japan to use a prosthetic arm and she also became a Paralympic athlete. Manami placed 4th in the Women's 100 meter Breaststroke in 2008, and placed 8th in the same event in 2012.

Thanks to a prosthesis that was designed specifically to enable Manami to hold her violin bow, she is able to play the violin again. She now travels Japan, lecturing and performing for audiences of all ages.

Thank you, Manami Ito, for your perseverance and for sharing your talents with the world!

# Aretha Franklin
## *Singer*

Aretha was born in 1942, and began singing gospel music as a child at the church where her father served as a pastor. Her professional career started when she was 12 years old and she began touring the country with her father as he gave sermons. As they traveled and met people in the music industry, Aretha became certain that singing was her passion. She moved to New York when she was 18, and was signed to her first record deal. Over time, Aretha became a singing sensation with hits like, "Respect," and "(You Make Me Feel Like) A Natural Woman," and in the 1960's she was crowned the Queen of Soul.

Aretha Franklin has received  many awards including the Presidential Medal of Freedom, the National Medal of Arts, and she was the first female artist to be inducted into the Rock and Roll Hall of Fame.

Aretha used her voice to serve as an icon for black women everywhere, and has inspired young female artists for decades. She was considered a civil rights activist and a humanitarian, and she was said to be a symbol of black equality.

Thank you, Aretha Franklin, for sharing your music and your passionate voice!

# Kristin Chenoweth
## *Performer*

Adopted when she was just five days old, Kristin Chenoweth was raised by two chemical engineers in Oklahoma. Her love for the arts began at an early age when she would sing gospel songs at churches in her community. She performed in school plays and musicals, and decided to study musical theatre and operatic performance in college.

After graduation, Kristin starred in many performances and eventually made her Broadway debut in 1997. From there, she rocketed to stardom, releasing albums, making television appearances, starring in films, and of course, singing and acting on Broadway. While she's famous for many roles, her most well-known might be as Glinda the Good Witch in the Broadway musical, "Wicked."

Winning multiple awards for her singing and acting, Kristin has used her fame to create Kristin Chenoweth's Broadway Bootcamp. Students in grades 8-11 work on their singing, dancing, and acting skills under the tutelage of famous stars and industry professionals, like herself. The students learn the value of arts and share what they have learned at the end of the bootcamp through a live performance.

Thank you, Kristin Chenoweth, for sharing your passion for the arts with future generations!

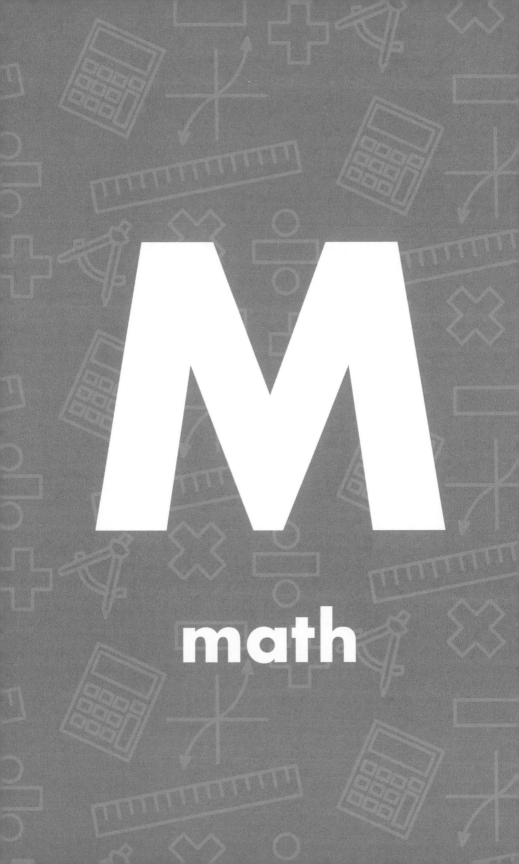

# M

## math

**"Mathematics may not teach us how to add love and to subtract hate, but it gives us hope that every problem has a solution. We just need to find it."**
*Roger W. Davis*

Mathematics involves numbers, equations, algorithms, and formulas to solve problems. By quantifying the world around us, we can count, measure, graph, and forecast solutions to the issues we face everyday. The following mathematicians made strides in gender equality, space travel, and the United States' economy.

# Katherine Johnson
## *Computer*

Katherine Johnson was drawn to mathematics at an early age. She skipped many grades in school, and eventually became one of three Black students to attend West Virginia University for graduate school. She was hired at NASA (formerly NACA) as a computer — someone who manually computes all of the numbers into all of the formulas to ensure the programs would run smoothly. Katherine was so good at her job, that before John Glenn went up in Friendship 7, he requested that she run the numbers first and refused to blast off until she gave the 'all clear.'

Katherine's story was depicted in the film "Hidden Figures," where it displays the obstacles she had to overcome. It shows how she successfully overcame every single obstacle and truly thrived, ultimately progressing the STEAM fields to be more equitable for all.

Thank you, Katherine Johnson, for your contributions to mathematics, to aeronautics, and for helping progress both gender and racial equality!

# Sophie Germain
## *Mathematician*

Sophie Germain was a French mathematician, who famously taught herself differential calculus while France was suffering through the Reign of Terror.

She wrote to the popular professors and mathematicians of the time, requesting lecture notes and submitting papers under the pseudonym "Monsieur LeBlanc," for she feared her learning would be stifled due to the societal concept that studying math was considered "dangerous" for women. She corresponded with Lagrange and Gauss, notable mathematicians, who encouraged her academics and discoveries in the realm of math.

Sophie was enthralled with number theory, she won an award for her mathematics skills from the French Academy of Sciences in 1816 and proved Fermat's Last Theorem in 1825.

Thank you, Sophie Germain, for your contributions to the field of mathematics and for inspiring girls around the world. You have shown that even in the face of adversity, everyone can accomplish their dreams!

# Georgia Neese Clark Gray
## *Economist*

Georgia was born in Richland, Kansas in 1898. She was always good with numbers, and excelled in math at school, so she decided to major in economics at Washburn University. After graduation, however, she decided to pursue acting, and moved to New York City. Georgia became friends with many notable actors and actresses, like Charlie Chaplin and Helen Hayes, and was a successful actress for about a decade.

When her father got sick, she returned to Kansas to take over the family businesses, ranging from general stores to real estate. She eventually became president of the Richland State Bank (now Capital City Bank). Georgia was involved in local, state and federal politics, and was considered to be well-liked and a very articulate representative of Kansas' Democratic Party.

Thanks to her head for business and aptitude for mathematics, Georgia Neese Clark Gray became the first female Treasurer of the United States, and her signature can be found on any bills that were released into circulation from 1949-1953.

Thank you, Georgia, for your contributions to business and mathematics, and for being an inspiration to the next generation!

# YOU!

Just like the women who have come before you, you have the opportunity to be an innovator in the fields of science, technology, engineering, arts, and math.

Let's Go Full STEAM Ahead!

**To learn more about STEAM education, visit www.letsgofullSTEAMahead.com**

On the website, you will find additional biographies of innovators in STEAM, as well as resources for STEAM activites. You can also nominate an influential woman in your own community to be honored during Women in STEAM Week, held annually during the third week in October.

# Acknowledgements

Thanks to Christian for reading my manuscript and for helping me learn keyboard shortcuts for Adobe so that I could make the illustations faster.

Thanks to Rob and Austin for looking over every single iteration of the illustrations when I decided to make one little change.

Thanks to Matt from Jimmy John's for delivering my #12 Beach Club with dijon mustard and bacon so promptly.

Thanks to my computer for not crashing during this process, I probably would have cried.

Thanks to all of the inspirational women who have paved the way for young women like me.

Thanks to all who educated me and empowered me to become and engineer and an advocate.

Most of all, thanks to my mom for everything.

# About the Author

Sierra Marie Bonn is an engineering student, a violinist, a designer, and an advocate for women in STEAM. She is the founder of "Let's Go Full STEAM Ahead!"an initiative to promote STEAM education and engagement, which empowers the next generation of scientists, technologists, engineers, artists, and mathematicians.

Made in the USA
Columbia, SC
02 December 2021

50179750R00029